Praise for the story behir

"Jonah, thank you for sharing your story at our annual Facebook conference last week. Your personal story, in addition to the success you've seen with Scene75, is inspiring and humbling. Though you told the story with a great deal of modesty and humor, you exemplify the personal and professional leadership that was the central theme of our two-day meeting. You really stole the show. I wish you the best of luck, and while we don't have an office in Dayton, you did gain 1,300+ fans rooting for your success."

—David Fischer, vice president of business and marketing partnerships at Facebook

"Your story, your passion for your family and community, and generosity are incredibly inspiring, Jonah. In two packed days of presentations, many from professional speakers, you were my favorite. Thank you for sharing your story and for helping other business owners."

—John Yi, manager, marketing technology developers at Pinterest and former global head of marketing technology partnerships at Facebook

"On behalf of everyone at Facebook I want to say THANK YOU for sharing your story with us. You are an inspiration and the reason we come to work every day."

—Dan Levy, director of small business at Facebook

"One of the absolute highlights of the [Facebook Annual Global Sales] meeting—I have been telling everyone your great story. Family and community are so central to what we think about every day, and seeing it come to life on stage in your presentation was truly an inspiration to go back and do everything we can for everyone the platform serves!"

—Eva Saks Press, global business manager at Facebook

"Congrats to your success and opportunity, Jonah!! You are an inspiration to us who want to own our own business someday. Keep up the great work and thanks for the help you have given."

—Jarrod Shell, Scene75 Facebook fan

"Jonah, I live in Youngstown, Ohio, and Friday is my twenty-seventh birthday, and I plan on driving the 250-mile trip just to celebrate it at Scene75 with my girlfriend, older sister, and brother-in-law. I just wanted to say thank you for building such a great establishment."

—Lee Phillips, Scene75 Facebook fan

"Jonah, you were amazing! Thank you for sharing your story with us and inspiring us all to lead."

—Joanna Bursch, global business manager at Facebook

"My role model."

"An incredible story and an amazing presentation. Thanks for sharing your story with us, and for teaching us about what the Facebook platform can (and should) do."

"You are an amazing person for writing and telling your customers how much you appreciate them! Something you don't see or hear very often!! Congratulations on your success, and I am sure you will succeed in anything you do!!"

"Congrats Jonah, one heck of a fun place and an owner that is just one of the team members. Nowhere else have I ever witnessed an owner so engaged with his customers and operations of his company."

How One Entrepreneur Captured the Hearts of a
Community and the Attention of Facebook

BEFORE THE
DOORS OPENED

Published by Scene75 Entertainment

ISBN-10: 0692027491
ISBN-13: 978-0-692-02749-3

Acknowledgments

To the fans of Scene75 Entertainment Center: You are the ONLY reason Scene75 has been successful, and you are the ONLY reason I have this story to share. For that, I am forever grateful. Thank you for making my dream a reality and for continuing to support Scene75 to keep that dream alive—not only on my behalf but also on behalf of my team, the other guests, and the city of Dayton. The journey has only begun. It is truly my life's honor to have you on it with me.

To my teammates: Thank you for making Scene75 the exciting, welcoming and safe place that it is. Your passion for our brand, our guests, and your roles inspires me daily. Thank you for accepting my vision and for helping Scene75 reach its fullest potential.

To the team at Facebook: Thank you for developing the platform that allowed me to share my story in a way that resonated with my fans. Your platform amazes me. Dan Levy, thank you for writing the foreword to this book and for allowing me the privilege of speaking at Facebook's annual sales meeting and of serving on Facebook's inaugural Small and Medium Business Council.

To my family and friends: Thank you for supporting my journey. You are the backbone of this book as you are the backbone of my life.

Foreword

"You've got to meet Jonah," my colleague Elisabeth told me. "Jonah wrote a brave letter to Zuck [Mark Zuckerberg] sharing his personal story and his business's success with Facebook ads."

Having just started a new role responsible for helping small businesses succeed on Facebook, I was intrigued. And I was looking to meet clients. So I called Jonah.

My first conversation with Jonah was not the lay-up "thank you" I expected. Jonah shared deep gratitude, but also real criticism and feedback. Listening to his passion, I realized that I was not in an ordinary job. And Jonah was not an ordinary customer.

Since our first conversation, our relationship deepened. Jonah hosted one of our team members at one of his regular 'Facebook education' events. He spoke to more than 1,000 Facebook employees at our annual sales conference, moving many to tears with his family story about Scene75. And he joined our inaugural SMB council to help us shape the future of Facebook. And that is just the part I have seen. He has told me about awards he has won for his work with Scene75 and his continuing business success.

Today, our team at Facebook serves more than one million small business advertisers. The number is staggering. And that is why Jonah is so important to me: he taught me about the people behind the numbers. He is the example I use when I talk with new hires to show how their work can impact others. He is the reminder of why we created Facebook in the first place —

because the Internet can be about real people, human stories, authentic emotions, and the ability to change lives personally and in business.

It is also why this is such an important book. Because people all over the world ask me about how Facebook can work to help their businesses. And beyond Facebook, how they as small business owners can effect positive change in their communities. And I always reply the same way — I have a friend who taught me it is possible.

After two years of conversation, disagreements, laughs, and sharing our heartfelt stories in front of thousands, I am most proud to call Jonah a friend.

—Dan Levy, director of small business at Facebook

Introduction

Passion. It is a powerful emotion capable of awakening the dormant giant within each of us. It is the key that unlocks our latent potential, pushing us to extremes. Yet, often, we deliberately turn our backs to it. We pursue careers in which passion rarely enters the equation; we allow routine in our daily lives to trump the pursuit of greatness; we fear leaving our comfort zones even while we remain dissatisfied with current choices.

Mark Albion, author, consultant, and former Harvard Business School professor, discussed a study on passion and work in his book titled *Making a Living, Making a Life*. The study, conducted by Srully Blotnick from 1960 to 1980, comprised 1,500 business school graduates who fell into one of two distinct groups. "Group A contained the individuals who selected their first job on the basis of money, believing that they would get to their passions later in their career. 83% or 1,245 of the people studied fell in to Group A. The remaining 17%, or 255 subjects, elected to find work that they were passionate about regardless of money. At the conclusion of this 20-year study, 101 of the subjects were multi-millionaires. Group A produced one (1) of the 101. The other 100 came from the group of individuals who chose to follow their passion." (Albion, 2000)

I learned about this study in 2007 as an MBA student at the University of Chicago Booth School of Business, and it has had a profound impact on my life ever since. You see, as a first-year MBA student, I was unquestionably a Group A student who wanted what a high percentage of my classmates wanted most — a high-paying job. I turned to investment banking for my summer internship, knowing that successful completion would lead to a full-time, six-figure salary and a signing bonus. What I never imagined was that the market was on the verge of collapsing. Once-illustrious financial institutions would disappear overnight, and my colleagues would see their coveted job offers vanish before their eyes. My personal experience was perhaps even more unexpected — half of my summer colleagues were fired on the same day the firm offered a full-time position to me upon graduating that fall. It was at that moment that I realized I needed a better understanding of myself and of the uncertainties of the future. If banking were my passion, I wondered, would I be willing to subject myself to the uncertainty my colleagues had just experienced at the hand of another? No, I was not willing to do so. With that decided, what was I truly passionate about in life? The answer did not come easily to me, but once I figured it out, veering from my path was not an option. My passion became the reason I woke up each morning. I became a Group B student, and passion guided my journey.

To understand my pursuit of passion, or more accurately, my calling, is to understand the creation of Scene75 Entertainment Center. And to understand that journey is to understand the evolution of Scene75's Facebook page. On the pages that follow, you will learn about me and my facility and a great deal about how I attracted fans by the tens of thousands to my business's page. I hope doing so will serve as an inspiration to you so you too can achieve your dreams, even those, like mine, that start with less than a one-percent chance of coming to fruition.

Chapter 1

My name is Jonah, and I am an entrepreneur — or in layman's terms, a crazy-ass fool.

All joking aside, entrepreneurship is not for the fainthearted. It is perhaps the longest, most inverted roller coaster ride of one's lifetime, in which sometimes the ups are mistaken for the downs, and perhaps more frequently, the downs are mistaken for the ups.

Entrepreneurship requires a plateful of wits, strategy, planning, diligence, and hard work, along with heaping side portions of both risk and luck. Some say entrepreneurs are born. Perhaps. Others say entrepreneurship can be learned. Perhaps. I, however, firmly believe it is a calling. I do not necessarily mean this in a divine sort of way, but rather in a "This is what I should be doing at this point in time, and nothing will impede me from reaching my goal" sort of way.

Every entrepreneur will face roadblocks along the journey. They are an integral part of the job description. Some roadblocks will require nothing more than a small hop to overcome — you will hardly know your progress was at risk. Other roadblocks will require a step stool — you will be able to see your destination clearly, but you will need to dig deeper within yourself to reach it. And yet others will require a fully outstretched ladder — you won't be able to see your destination, and at times you will even wonder if it is still there. Another intangible obstacle, and perhaps one of the most difficult, will be the challenges posed by those who cannot comprehend your need to pursue your passion. The question at that pivotal point becomes whether you believe in your vision so much and whether you want to achieve your dream so earnestly that there is no direction worthy of your time but up; you are willing to make the longest, tallest climb of your life on what very well may prove to be an unstable ladder. It should be so vividly apparent that the climb is all but necessary to your well-being and to who you are as a person that you are willing to do whatever it takes to achieve the goal despite the potential of falling.

A few months before I turned 27 years old, after several years of management consulting, investment banking, and rigorous preparation for the CFA exams, my calling toward entrepreneurship became so apparent that no other option in the world, including a six-figure paycheck, could divert my attention. I was all in. And in my case, the journey started with a need for an extendable ladder.

This is my story.

Chapter 2

I grew up in a suburb of Cincinnati, Ohio. I lived in the same household as my mom and dad, my sister, and my grandma — yes, my grandma. My aunts, uncles, and cousins, as well as their children, all lived in town, with some living next door to us. We were a very close family, and from an early age, I learned that this familial bond was more important to me than anything else in my life. They were my best friends, my harshest critics, and more often than not, my most staunch supporters.

My dad is a numismatist turned real estate developer with a penchant for risk. An entrepreneur all of his life, my dad taught me at an early age how to seek out a niche and make it my own — a skill he practiced at some times more successfully than others. My mom, a conservative woman, finds utmost pleasure in volunteering and in cooking three-course meals for thirty. She taught me that sometimes our greatest joys and our deepest sources of happiness in life come from what we do for others. My sister, who is only one year older than I am, is a creative being with a penchant for producing art; I only wish I were half as talented and as smart as she.

From left: Mom, Dad, Me, Sister

And my grandma, well, she is a hoot. Bub, as I call her, owned a gourmet popcorn store throughout my childhood and put my sister and me to work at the ripe ages of 7 and 6 years old, respectively. Bub's way of teaching me responsibility at an early age was to identify the worst job in her entire store and to make sure that I mastered it through repetition; though thin, wimpy and most definitely underage for the hours I contributed, I was a bona fide all-star when it came to the ever-important role of discarding unpopped kernels from freshly popped popcorn! And yet somehow, she would find a renegade kernel or two and reprimand me because I missed them. When I finally graduated from the kernel conundrum, she assigned me to a dark, musty warehouse to assemble shipping boxes by the thousands. At one point, I thought about jumping into one of my perfectly assembled, corrugated beauties to ship myself out of there, but before I had a chance to find one large enough, I was off to Bub's next challenge. When I was in junior high school, Bub insisted on grilling me with flashcards before tests, only to ask me with utter seriousness, and a bit of frustration, why I only scored 96 percent on one test instead of 100 percent. Bub was tough. But she was also the most loving grandma one could have.

Bub and I

The memories I share of my family are among the most salient of my life, and they are the backdrop and motivation for the story in the pages to come. Growing up, I knew that they were important in my life. But it wasn't until I was grown up that I realized that, in many ways, they *are* my life.

Perhaps in part due to Bub's nudging, I graduated near the top of my class at all levels of education. I graduated summa cum laude in 2000 from Sycamore High School. I then followed in my sister's footsteps and joined her at Washington University in St. Louis, where I graduated summa cum laude in 2004 with a bachelor's degree in business. And after a three-year stint in management consulting and completion of the CFA exams, I returned to school at the University of Chicago Booth School of Business, where I graduated with honors with an MBA in 2009.

Through intense study and preparation, I set myself up to be what I thought I always wanted to be — a highly desirable job candidate who could secure a role at the highest salary range among my peers. And I did just that. I was finally going to reap the rewards from pushing so hard during the prior dozen or so years of my life. By almost all standards, I had officially made it and was about to live what I envisioned to be the true American Dream.

Now, don't get me wrong, along with writing about my many successes, I could just as easily include my failures at each of these levels of education, but life, in all honesty, was going well for me. Living in a bachelor pad in a building overlooking Lake Michigan, I had a close circle of friends and a girlfriend who adored me. It appeared to be a perfect storm of bliss for a soon-to-be 27-year-old.

Yet, possessing all of this, I felt strangely empty inside. While the idea of living well in the great city of Chicago excited me and was unquestionably the desired outcome of my life's endeavors, I felt a calling of a very different nature. One evening, after much deliberation and an analysis of my deepest values, I decided to leave it all—everything. I turned down the high-profile job offer, kicking aside that promise of financial stability and wealth, and in the process, I later lost the girlfriend I loved.

So, the question you are asking now is, "Why did he do it?" Or maybe that's the second question after, "Is he a crazy-ass fool?" What on earth could inspire a person to set aside what was essentially the promise of a greater tomorrow, particularly after deliberately working so hard to get there? The answer? Family.

Chapter 3

My family, one of my greatest passions in life, was struggling. In particular, my parents were facing dire financial difficulties. As parents, they like to show eternal strength and fortitude to my sister and me; they see it as their foremost duty. But sometimes even the strongest people show weaknesses — they are, after all, only human. And weaknesses, I'm afraid, abounded.

While I was living well in graduate school, my dad was facing the weakest economy he had seen in his thirty-plus years as a real estate developer. Dayton, where he primarily developed, was hit particularly hard by the widespread economic downturn. Plots of land became nearly worthless overnight as residential growth slowed and then stopped. Commercial properties failed to attract new tenancies as few businesses wished to enter the market; current tenants faced extreme difficulty upholding their commitments to their landlords. Worse yet, obtaining financing became all but impossible as banks called in their loans and personal lines of credit disappeared. While I was enjoying the perfect bliss of good fortune, my family was living the perfect storm of calamity.

My dad was left with several vacant properties and no prospective tenants — and time was working against him. My family could not afford to keep these properties vacant any longer. Bankruptcy was creeping closer.

After several phone conversations with my dad, and with a newfound understanding of myself, I decided that it was time to make a decision. That decision would likely shape my world for the rest of my life … and it would not in the least guarantee a better life.

I stood at the proverbial fork in the road as two very distinct paths unfolded before me. The first, staying on the present journey and trying to make the best life for myself with the job offer I had received, seemed logical, but extremely selfish. The second, changing course and moving back to Ohio to try to help my family *somehow*, seemed selfless to me — which I valued to a great degree — but it also seemed extremely nebulous and full of risk. Not only were my parents struggling, I might have struggled right beside them. Even riskier, perhaps, was the thought that venturing down this path would likely make it difficult for me to return to my former career course in the event my efforts in Ohio failed. I surmised it would be much harder to find a job as a *failure* than as a newly minted MBA graduate!

Any attempt at well thought-out analysis, however, was short-lived. I did not see how I could try to make a career for myself knowing that my family was struggling back home. I felt my calling — a calling that only I could answer and a calling that would lead me to entrepreneurship. It was a calling that burned within me; it burned so deeply within me that I knew of no better use for my time. In fact, it became so clear to me that this was the right choice that, frankly, I saw it as the *only* choice, no matter the chance of failure. I wanted to help. And I wanted to help in a big way. The question was *how*.

Chapter 4

A few weeks before completing my MBA and moving back to Ohio, I stayed awake late each night working in the university's main library. While those around me were studying for upcoming exams or finishing school projects, I had already shifted gears to my first course of action for my imminent move back home. I wanted to develop a vacant parcel of land that my family owned into a miniature golf course. Odd choice, I know. But I wanted to focus my attention on family entertainment, as I had noticed a void in the Dayton market. Furthermore, when I looked at the opportunity through the lens of an MBA student, I felt that a typical brick-and-mortar retail business would be at greater risk with each passing day, considering the proliferation of mobile devices and online shopping. I wanted to create something that would serve a long-standing need and take advantage of people's social behavior. No matter how advanced in-home electronics might become or how much our lives might be shaped by online interactions, I believe that people will always have a desire to explore, eat, socialize and entertain in person. Thus, my thesis began, and with it, my first of many drawings.

With meager artistic talent and scant supplies, I designed Putters Par-adise miniature golf course, one hole after another. I tapped into my memories of the many miniature golf courses I had played as a child (a longtime favorite hobby of mine), recalling the holes that had left a memorable mark on my childhood. And though I am certainly not an architect, I applied these memories to what I ultimately wanted the course to become. I then put this vision on paper. (I did mention my sister was the artist, didn't I?)

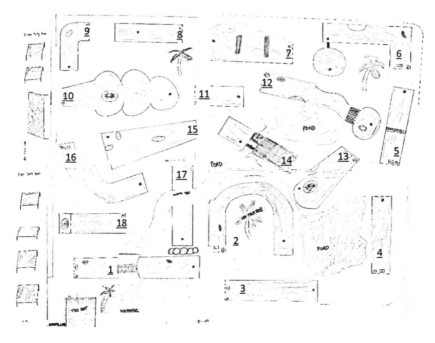

An early sketch of Putters Par-adise

When I finally ventured back to Ohio, I shared my rudimentary drawings with Dusty, the owner of an excavation company my family used for its real estate projects. After miraculously securing funding from a local bank (which is another book in itself), Dusty and I worked together to build the reality from the drawing, marking the construction of my first entertainment project and the first and only miniature golf course Dusty ever built.

Putters Par-adise was named a perennial winner of the best of six courses in Dayton. Visitors loved the course! They found it uniquely challenging, and they also appreciated the finer details that many area courses seemed to overlook — tropical music, beautiful landscaping, a free Hawaiian lei with each round, unique putting (and singing) competitions, and tournaments with coveted prizes.

Putters Par-adise, by day and by night

Creating a miniature golf course was not my end game; I had much bigger visions for what I wanted to build in Dayton. But it was a great starting point for my entry into the family entertainment industry. Operating the course was also a great learning opportunity. I quickly realized that any future entertainment efforts in Dayton would require an indoor setting, as sunny months are few and far between; if it happens to rain on a Saturday, one had better be prepared to eat Ramen daily that week. Putters Par-adise was my first stepping-stone to future adventures.

Within a month of the course's opening, I ambitiously leaped to the next entertainment project — an indoor project — to occupy family-owned real estate. It would be the first video gaming theater in the country, the Chaos Room, and it opened later that same year, about 45 minutes away.

Chaos Room, gaming theater and arcade

With a mix of next-generation gaming consoles and state-of-the-art arcade cabinets, the facility impressed industry veterans who had been in the amusement business for decades. However, I quickly learned a few critical lessons from the Chaos Room. One, it is extremely challenging to achieve success in the industry as a single-faceted entertainment operation—the cross-dynamic of multiple attractions is an important revenue driver. Two, Dayton residents were starving for entertainment options; they valued that the Chaos Room was a locally owned business, and they appreciated the high level of service my team provided. And three, Facebook had the potential to be an incredibly powerful marketing tool. Although I had an e-mail database of thousands of guests at the Chaos Room, e-mail open rates were low, and perhaps more significantly, e-mail failed to provide a constant flow of two-way communication. I believed Facebook could solve both of these issues, and if used strategically, it could even help create a brand *prior* to that brand's existence.

While pushing the Putters Par-adise and Chaos Room operations forward, I developed plans for the project that was the true catalyst for my move back to Ohio—Scene75 Entertainment Center. But Scene75 was merely a dream, a piein-the-sky idea with less than a one percent chance of succeeding. Sources of funding for what looked like at least a $5 million project were extremely limited; city-imposed zoning was excruciatingly painful to modify; the learning curve was steep; few believed in Dayton; and even fewer believed in the vision.

Furthermore, few saw potential in the physical building. It had been dormant for years, with few, if any, real estate inquiries; numerous prior tenants had failed in the location. Geographically, it was 20 minutes north of Dayton's "sweet spot," situated on the far less desirable side of the interstate. And perhaps most troubling to potential partners who toured the building, support columns were placed relatively close together, making it nearly impossible for people to see the development potential, particularly when discussing a concept that involved go-karts racing among these columns.

6196 Poe Avenue, pre-construction of Scene75 Entertainment Center

Yet considering the possibility of what could be and how much I knew I had given up to try to help my family, I continued to push forward against all odds. I saw Scene75, which would occupy the largest of my family's vacant properties, as an opportunity to rescue my family financially while also creating something unique and influential for the community. For those reasons, I knew of no higher calling for the use of my time. The vision was set, and win or lose, only one path lay ahead.

For the following three years, I dedicated my life to the mission of creating Scene75. I visited more than one hundred entertainment facilities across the country, and I attended one industry seminar after another. I met with existing operators at every chance possible; I negotiated deals with manufacturers that they had never before considered; I attracted key financial and operating partners. Because I could not afford the expense of a formal set of blueprints by an acclaimed entertainment architect, let alone the suggested structural changes to the building, I designed the facility myself with my father's oversight, with my uncle as the general contractor, and with the assistance of a local architect. As a result of years of steadfast effort, Scene75, which was set to become the largest indoor entertainment center in the nation, was finally going to exist.

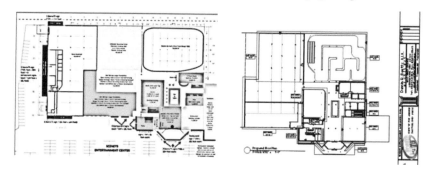

Early renderings of Scene75 Entertainment Center

Chapter 5

As final plans began to take shape and the interior demolition and build-out began (without removing a single column), I sent an initial press release to local media contacts who had covered the opening of Putters Par-adise and the Chaos Room. Within a few days, news organizations flocked to the story. After all, my partners and I had just announced that Dayton would soon be home to the largest indoor entertainment center in the country!

The construction of Scene75 received front-page newspaper coverage and was featured on several prime time television broadcasts. We were a breaking news story in the local business journal. And we were featured in numerous local print publications. But despite this great publicity — publicity, in truth, that any business owner could only dream about for his or her new business — my brand was practically unrecognizable. No buzz, no energy, no magic, no hoopla, and little, if any, noticeable community fanfare.

My partners, rightfully, were terrified. We were only a few months away from opening a 124,000-square-foot facility (with potential to expand an additional 40,000 square feet), and it seemed as though no one actually cared! Our marketing budget, which we had once believed would begin at $50,000, a relatively limited amount for the scope of the project, was now $10,000 — yes, $10,000 — due to construction cost overruns. The marketing budget was a mere fraction of what many successful first-rate facilities in this industry typically spend each year.

What could I do? After much deliberation, I informed my team of partners that I intended to allocate our entire marketing budget of $10,000 to Facebook advertisements. They looked at me, understandably, in shock and with great skepticism. My partner, Pete, who had recently retired after selling several of his local car dealerships, was accustomed to spending *$80,000 per month* on advertising campaigns. Pete did not see how $10,000 in total marketing expenditures for a project of Scene75's proportions could be effective, let alone using all of that on a virtual tool. In fact, when I had first presented the initial $50,000 marketing budget to Pete, that line item was the one and only budget figure that he had challenged as being too low!

Though I was admittedly somewhat skeptical of our ability to make an impact with only $10,000, I knew that Facebook at least offered us an opportunity to *try* to attract loyal supporters, who in turn could help Scene75 garner the attention of others. From brief experiments with the Chaos Room, I knew that $10,000 in radio, television or print advertising would buy far too little exposure to successfully launch our business. Moreover, my goal was not to provide one-time exposure to Scene75, like most of these media outlets offered. My goal was to create an ongoing relationship with individuals in the community whom I could touch not only today, upon the release of my words, but tomorrow and the next day, as additional words followed.

I felt that my only hope for the $10,000 to have a legitimate impact was a viral explosion. I needed to find enough people to support my dream to develop some form of critical mass and make a meaningful impact. Essentially, *my* dream needed to become *our* dream if we were to succeed.

So I rolled the dice on Facebook advertisements, and the move paid off in a very big way, surpassing my expectations. Over a three-month time frame, all during the construction phase of Scene75, I grew our fan base to 23,000 local fans prior to opening our doors for business. Our fan base surged at a maximum rate of 700 new fans in a single day! Thanks to Facebook and its ability to spread my words so rapidly while also allowing me to keep a community engaged, Scene75 became such a recognizable brand that people would stop me at gas stations and at restaurants upon seeing the logo on my shirt, long before we opened. And more often than not, these apparent strangers would tell me that they admired my passion and my humility, and that they genuinely looked forward to reading my personal and amusing Facebook posts each day. Many such fans knew me by name.

It was a surreal experience, yet it was undeniably real. And it seemed that every time I posted to the Scene75 Facebook page, the number of fans grew; every time that number grew, more people would flock to our page as existing fans shared it with friends of their own. As Allison S. expressed in a Facebook post one month prior to opening, "Can't go anywhere without hearing about this!!!"

Being a topic of conversation and exposing a brand to the public was great, but the results ran even deeper than mere exposure and virtual fanfare. Through Facebook, I attracted numerous financial sponsors who believed in what we were doing, even though they had yet to see a finished product. They saw the excitement on our Facebook page, felt a connection to my posts and wanted to support my journey—

whether through sponsored banners surrounding the sand volleyball courts, digital advertisements on displays within the facility, or discounted products. Furthermore, before we poured the sand for our sand volleyball courts, one of two outdoor attractions of our facility, we attracted 89 volleyball teams for a single summer league, which represented nearly 400 people who would be visiting the facility every week during our opening months. Additionally, I attracted extremely passionate individuals who wanted to join the mission as Scene75 team members; many, inspired by my Facebook posts, felt a higher calling to contribute to the cause. They felt the truth in my writing, felt the unbridled enthusiasm stemming from my words and from the comments of fans, and felt a desire to be a part of whatever it was Scene75 would ultimately become. And all of this happened months before the doors opened.

I had hoped for a viral explosion, and Facebook was unequivocally the dynamite that I needed.

Chapter 6

So, how did I do it?

For me, Facebook was a canvas—a canvas on which I painted my personal journey for an entire community to see, feel, experience, and support. I *shared* my sacrifices, my failures, my successes, and my embarrassments. In doing so, I built an incredibly strong, engaged, and most important, local community who could physically support the end product that I was marketing.

As I quickly recognized, each fan count was a person behind a virtual page; though represented by a number, that number was actually a mother, a father, a teacher, a teenager, or a grandparent, among others. I knew that if I could appeal to that person's heart, I would not only grow the page count, I would also become an interesting topic of conversation at family dinner tables, business meetings, and casual get-togethers across town—an effect that never shows up in Facebook metrics but is undeniably powerful. I did not always write what I wanted to deliver; I wrote what I felt my fans genuinely wanted to read. I wanted to build an emotional tie.

So I shared all. I really did. Upon creating some posts, I had moments when I hesitated before tapping *Enter* on my keyboard, fearing that the truth I was revealing was either too true for my future guests to know or was so personal that I felt I was disclosing too much of myself to the world. The boundary between personal and virtual no longer existed; this was my community, and I was going to let them in on all aspects of Scene75—including my most personal thoughts.

More often than not, these posts created the greatest fanfare; my fans saw that I was exposing far more on Facebook than they had ever imagined a business owner would reveal, and their loyalty to my page, and thus their loyalty to my soon-to-open business, only increased with each new post. As I shared months prior to opening:

> "An interesting aspect about this Facebook page is that I'm actually a private person—I prefer life that way. I enjoy my quiet moments to reflect on life inwardly and rarely find a need to express thoughts outwardly. But I realized about a month ago (sometime around our hitting 5,000 fans, all prior to opening) that the journey of my last several years was no longer my own and that you all deserve to be included in my thoughts, particularly those pertaining to Scene75. My path has quickly transpired to be our journey. We as a community are now in this together—to keep this place, once we open, safe, clean, and family friendly. My team will certainly do its part (and I will personally hold them and myself accountable to give Scene75 our best), but it's up to ALL of us to help Scene75 reach its fullest potential. I have faith that we can do this—I wouldn't have jumped in the ocean head first, at least not without my swimmies, had I believed otherwise. Looking forward to the weeks ahead ... "

I unveiled my passion. I shared the victories, taking fans along with me. I showed them that I am human. I shared the struggle of starting a business, let alone one of Scene75's proportions. And I showed both my strengths and my weaknesses, no matter how uncomfortable at times this sharing made me feel. I took them along on the journey with me, a journey that only I could share. I made them feel as though they too were getting ready to open the largest indoor entertainment facility in the country, while showing them exactly how we were unique from all other entertainment centers. In doing so, I was providing subtle reasons why fans should rally behind us and provide support:

> "I spent half of this busy day calling the first group of thirty new hires directly. I wanted to speak to them personally and share my enthusiasm for inviting them to the team. Scene75 — we do things differently around here!"

I fought for the attention of my fans, and I worked hard to keep it. I shared anecdotes that would leave some crying, some laughing, and others in total amazement that a business owner was being so truthful. Through this, I quickly realized that my content was becoming my competitive advantage.

I created unique content via Facebook that my fans could not get in any other way. I made elements of my journey legendary, sometimes bringing up the same topic of conversation in a post the following week or month, if it had resonated with fans initially. I played with them whenever opportunity struck:

> "For all of my loyal readers … I'm thinking Kathleen [a name loyal readers recognized due to her frequent posts to the page] must be out of town. I did not get my "you are SO cute" comments this week! Missing her already and have yet to meet her!"

> "You are in luck folks. My dad [whom I often mentioned as being a bit behind modern times] relinquished his duties on the electronic prizes in the display case. In with the PS3,

PS Vita, Tablet, and Kindle Fire. Out with the cassette player! Haha. Love ya, Dad."

Whereas many businesses on Facebook, particularly larger corporations, tend to share content almost exclusively in matter-of-fact formats (e.g. "Open today 12 to 8 p.m.," "Shirts on sale," "We value our guests"), they are often representing the interests of others. As a small-business owner, I was able to get up close and personal and represent myself, without fear of overstepping corporate boundaries — a *huge* competitive advantage of small businesses. I learned that fans tend not to share posts that are mundane or ordinary, or that could be equally represented in a newspaper. To be the talk of the town and to be shared from person to person on Facebook, to reach that desired viral stardom, I had to be different. I lived on the edge. The more unique and touching my posts became, the more eager my fans were to share. I totally owned my Facebook page. It was my home court, and I took the time to shape it into what I ultimately wanted it to become. I was personal, yet I was professional. I shared myself and unveiled my personality, but I did so in a way that brought people closer to who I am as a person and what I wanted my business to ultimately represent. The following post garnered 534 likes and 124 comments:

"… I have given up much on the personal front to get to this point, but the support you have shown makes me wonder if perhaps it was all actually worth it. I love what our team is doing here. I think you will be THRILLED to find a facility such as Scene75 here in Dayton; I know no other facility like this. But it hasn't been easy. Along the journey, many said that it wouldn't work, or rather, that it couldn't work ... yet in a few weeks, they will see so much more than they likely ever envisioned. I am so happy to have received the support from you all to date. It means SO MUCH to me. I am an ordinary guy. Truly. I just took a chance and had a lot of people along the way who believed in ME as a person, more so perhaps than they even believed in this project. To call this path anything other than a journey would be inaccurate. We have leaped so many hurdles to bring this project to the point it is today that it would take me days to explain. But we are getting there. Within a matter of weeks (I hope), Scene75 will welcome you with open arms. And I personally look forward to meeting you at the door."

At times, I found that I broke the guidelines of posting "best practices." I was actually advised by a Facebook contact to limit the length of my posts to obtain optimal results on mobile devices. But it seemed that the more I wrote, the better the response from my fans, not necessarily because my posts were long (I imagine the Facebook contact is correct), but rather because people genuinely *wanted* to read what I had to write. They craved my writing.

As Craig E. posted, "Keep up the great work. Love following your posts and keeping track of your whole process of building and opening such an awesome business. Can't wait to spend some time in what I believe will be a great place to help put Dayton back on the map."

They were so into the journey of creating Scene75 and the personal *Jonah* stories I shared that they would sometimes ask me to post more often ... and I was already posting as many as three times a day on days when I did post! As Amy A. wrote,

"I've been missing your daily posts, I need some inspiration."

I posted not according to any rule, but whenever I experienced something worthy of sharing with my fans. I posted when inspiration struck, not when the clock dictated that it was time.

As Melissa B. posted one month prior to opening, "Yes, yes, I'm all excited for the opening along with the 11K+ others … however, all on its own, this Facebook page is a lot of fun too."

Due to the results I was enjoying, I treated Scene75's Facebook page like gold. Intentionally, I was the only one with access to our page. I did not want anyone, no matter how well-intentioned, to do anything that could possibly disturb the community relationship I had worked so hard to build. I took the time, no matter how much work I had on my plate, to respond to everyone and everything on the page. I shocked fans with not only thorough but also timely and personal responses. Few could believe that the man putting together this mammoth project would take time out of his day to respond to them … and often to do so only a few minutes after they first posted. But I most certainly did!

Through these timely responses, I learned that by shocking fans, I created raving fans. I spent much time during the page's growth thinking about why this was the case, and as I reflected on my own experiences with the customer service departments of many corporations, the answer quickly became apparent. How many of us have called or e-mailed a company only to be put on hold for 20 minutes or to receive an e-mail response one week later, if at all? Most of us, I'm sure. And often, the answers are so contrived that you may as well not have called or e-mailed in the first place. Facebook, on the other hand, brings everything into the moment. It is a platform to differentiate for those willing to make the time to do so. And when you can stand apart from a pack of what I consider to be many mediocre guest experiences, you have a brilliant, and very public, moment to shine.

As Kathleen G. posted in May of 2012, two months prior to opening, "I love how you are taking the time to respond to all of the postings on here! I really love how honest you are with posters. You don't just tell them what they want to hear but give an honest answer with an explanation. So many "PR" people are full of "BS." You have my utmost respect!! Keep it up!!"

I showed fans that I cared from the deepest crevice of my heart. I showed them that this facility was not all for personal gain: it was for the betterment of a family, a community, and a city. I was one of them. No ego, no hidden agenda, no attitude—just an ordinary guy on a mission trying to give life, and the most important project of that life, his all.

I demonstrated enthusiasm and gratitude when fans commented, and I demonstrated humility and fortitude, even when naysayers ultimately jumped into the conversation. I was truthful and genuine, and I respected all opinions. I told them that I would make mistakes and that the project would not be flawless when it opened—it would require tweaking, patience and fan input—but that I was determined to work tirelessly until my soon-to-be team and I got it right. The following post received 418 likes and 56 supportive comments:

"As we get closer and closer to opening (and no, we still don't have a date as the power rests with the city), I'd like to inform you that we, much like any new business, will face our challenges. We WILL make mistakes, guaranteed. In fact, I'm pretty sure we will screw a few things up big time! We are not a corporate entity that has replicated this model 100 times — we learn as we go. So PLEASE accept my personal apologies in advance. We are a passionate group giving you our personal best; we will ultimately get it right and in doing so, hold ourselves and our team accountable. Amazing times await! Thanks for the support!"

My words struck a chord with my fans. On the rare occasion that a fan posted something negative, I took the opportunity to turn it into a positive with an army of fans on the page eager to support me; sometimes they were so supportive that I would be fifth in line to respond to a naysayer only minutes after the initial post originated! They stood behind me when I needed them most. For example, when one individual posted that Scene75 would never make it as "EVERYTHING dies in Dayton," my fans stormed onto the battlefield with the following post that received 256 likes, 22 shares and 48 heated comments:

"We read some comments recently about how anything that opens in Dayton is doomed from the get go. That mindset is certainly disturbing (and inaccurate given the strength of the Dragons [a local minor league baseball team that has set professional sports league records for consecutive sellouts]), but it only motivates us further to prove the naysayers wrong. You all are the best. Who is with us? Please help us and share our page. We want to show those who say that nothing can be successful here and those who don't even know about us who we are — we are

DAYTON!"

Every day we gained new fans, or as I like to call them, brand advocates, whom I confidently felt would support me and Scene75 through any high tide we were bound to face. In a very short time period, they had become my family.

As Jenna J. kindly shared: "You are doing such a great job Jonah and changing Dayton in so many ways! You and your establishment are the talk of the town. I hear about you every day in so many conversations. You made the right decision and keep making new ones every day. Don't hesitate and go with your feelings—always."

Chapter 7

With construction well underway and a community of advocates on our Facebook page, I now needed to train the new hires I had personally invited to bring my dream to life.

Plans moved along at what seemed like breakneck speed, spurred by the excitement and encouragement of Facebook fans who kept asking, "When do you open!?!" Even the new employees I had notified by phone regularly asked, "When, when, when?" Pressed for time, yet uncertain of our opening date because of construction and permit delays, my skeleton crew of eight and I threw together a week's worth of instruction for nearly 100 new hires.

On the first day of training, I hardly noticed my new teammates entering the facility to register. Instead I was, as usual, running around the facility with my smartphone in hand, keeping up with Facebook posts and assessing the construction status of attractions, all while mentally wondering how training could possibly prepare my new team for what was ahead.

Having no experience in opening a project of Scene75's magnitude, what could I tell them other than my story — the story I am sharing with you? How thoroughly did my core team, several of whom had worked at my other entertainment projects, know the scope of the business? After all, it was I who had researched and traveled the country visiting entertainment centers. It was I who had strategized with other professionals to gain insights. Yet this core team proved ready to go ... to do their job for me, for my dream. And while the building was not quite ready for occupancy, they helped me train our new teammates as though we were to open the following day.

Until recently, I was unaware of a dynamic coursing through the team during that initial week of training. I actually came close to losing several members of the incoming team; construction delays were clearly visible and several considered seeking jobs with more imminent start dates. But the passion I had shared through Facebook long before I had ever met my teammates encouraged them to trust me and the journey ahead. The following is what I learned from Jackie W., one of my teammates:

"I was so excited to have been hired to work in a totally foreign environment — formerly having worked in professional office settings where I wore dresses and heels and was supplied with all the work equipment to perform the expected duties. With that excitement as my platform, I could overlook the primitive sign-in procedure at an unattended table with scraps of paper and a few pens. As a few more young newbies straggled in, I could tell they were as nervous as I so I put on my big-girl attitude and began directing them to the meeting room. That activity quelled my own anxiety, and I was glad to have something to do. Finally, we were all seated in a poorly lit and unfinished future party room. But none of that mattered to us as we sat with anticipation. Then you, Jonah, walked quickly to the front of the room, and the buzzing among us slowed to silence.

"Then it began to happen. It all goes back to the passion. It goes back to Jonah's vulnerability. He shared his story. Somehow he infused his passion into us. He was unassuming, but he pushed forward with fearlessness and tenacity, and we all caught it like a transmitted disease. We, too, could do it! *This* was our first reality.

"Our second reality hit our eyes and ears with a great awakening. Are we really supposed to open in two weeks to the public?!? We whispered among ourselves, repeatedly, even though we barely knew each other: 'This is never going to happen in two months, let alone two weeks.' Saws and drills were breaking the airwaves; wires, cords, scraps, boards, and you name it were scattered, hung, and strung throughout the huge facility, creating a risky obstacle course. We murmured, 'Ain't no way! Jonah has no idea how far he has to go before we are ready.' Every day that we arrived for training the scene looked the same, and we continued to wag our heads—but not in the presence of a trainer. We just kept putting one foot in front of the other and reading the public's Facebook posts that were counting the days until the doors opened.

"A true dichotomy. Jonah's passion and adrenaline ran through our veins. We kept going. Fear and skepticism tried to convince us to bolt. But we stayed on the bandwagon! We did not want to get off even though we did not have a clue how it could work. We felt electrified. As a group we were engaged to a dream, and we all felt it."

Presenting to my team for the first time, in an unfinished party room

Facebook proved not only to help me win the hearts of fans but also the hearts of my teammates. My words energized. My passion stirred something within them. And my calm helped soothe them. We were going to open an incredible facility for the community of Dayton, and in the face of much uncertainty, we stood stronger as a team. We were going to finish building my dream *together* as tens of thousands of Facebook fans waited in anticipation.

Chapter 8

I like to consider the prior chapters the softer, yet by far the most important, aspects of Scene75's Facebook success. While I incorporated a number of additional tools to ignite my Facebook page, none of these would have been particularly meaningful without content that my fans wanted to read. As explained on Facebook to the tune of 127 likes and 16 comments:

> "[Members of] The Racing Place [the go-kart track within Scene75] were asked today how our Facebook page has received so many likes, particularly without even being open. My partner's response: 'Read the posts!' Haha. Thank you for joining me on what has been the most challenging, fun, stressful and exciting journey of my life. Can't wait for you all to soon see what we've been up to for the last 3 years."

Nevertheless, I will explain in this chapter one particular tool that I used to achieve explosive growth: paid Facebook advertising. Facebook continues to evolve, and what I write today regarding this tool may differ from what is available as you read this book. The primary value of this book, therefore, will likely be the inspiration it offers and the softer tools previously presented, elements that I imagine will be timeless in their effectiveness.

Advertisements simply accelerated the pace of my growth, exposing my page to more people in a relatively condensed period of time; they boosted my effectiveness, in both reach and in time to convert. Yet it was the content that encouraged those who were on the page to share it with others, and it is content that will likely remain key as Facebook evolves.

With the exception of growing the page by 700 fans in a single day, nothing that I have mentioned regarding Facebook marketing thus far required a monetary investment. But when I did spend money, I built very specific campaign strategies to attract potential future Scene75 guests to our page. Given the low cost of entry for each ad (a fifty-dollar investment provided me with enough insight), I was able to run multiple ads simultaneously to determine where ad expenditures appeared most effective. I experimented with different approaches, much like a scientist might do in a laboratory. And through these experiments, I found that the most effective advertising medium within Facebook, at least for my page, was a *sponsored story*.

For those unfamiliar with a sponsored story, at the time of my writing, this tool is essentially an ad that shows up on the right side of the targeted user's Facebook page—but the only information shown is the logo of the advertising entity, the name of the entity, and how many of that specific person's friends like that entity's Facebook page. No additional message is displayed to convert viewers to fans or to highlight a point of differentiation of the business. It is basically a logo and an indication of familiar popularity. It is remarkably simple—yet amazingly brilliant.

I equate a sponsored story to a promotional endorsement. It yields tremendous credibility and interest to the potential fan. If your best friend loves a new restaurant in town and tells you that you have to try it, I am willing to wager that your interest in trying that restaurant will rise, or at the very least, your curiosity will. The sponsored story acts in the same way, except that it has the inherent potential to be more powerful because of its far-reaching effect.

Though elementary in concept, sponsored stories do require a bit of strategic targeting. Whom do you wish to target? What specific audience? Again, experimentation is important to identify what will prove most effective for your specific entity, but some basic strategy still remains.

For Scene75, my primary objective was to target individuals who could take advantage of everything we offered — from sand volleyball, to birthday parties, to corporate outings, to the consumption of food and adult beverages. I felt that if I could target these particular individuals, I might be able to capture their date night spend, their event celebration spend, and for those with children, their family spend. Specifically, I ran a sponsored story that targeted individuals 21 years or older, who lived within 25 miles of Dayton, and who were not already connected to Scene75's Facebook page, but who had friends who were. I ran a similar sponsored story a few months later and extended my reach to those within 50 miles of Dayton, along with the same additional parameters. Each of these filters proved to be powerful in attracting a local audience, an audience that I believed would patronize Scene75's full suite of offerings upon our opening.

The chart that follows exhibits the campaign statistics for all paid Facebook activity from Scene75's pre-opening campaign — you'll note that it ran 11 percent over the intended $10,000 marketing budget, in part because I had a hard time turning off the campaign knowing how effectively it was working! If I had had more money to spend at that time, I undoubtedly would have let the campaign continue to run with more funds supporting it.

Creating an Advertisement Campaign

14,539,706 Impressions 37,625 Clicks 29,225 Actions 0.259% CTR $11,477.22 Spent $0.79 CPM $0.31 CPC

Date Range	Campaign	Ad Name	Impressions	Social Impressions	Social %	Clicks	Social Clicks	CTR	Social CTR	CPC	CPM	Spent	Actions	Page Likes
Lifetime	SCENE75_13 TO 17 WITHIN 25 MILES_FRIENDS CONNECTED	SPONSORED STORY	770,718	770,711	100.00%	1,786	1,786	0.232%	0.232%	0.23	0.54	$416.93	1,798	1,125
Lifetime	SCENE75_21+ WITHIN 25 MILES_FRIENDS CONNECTED	SPONSORED STORY	3,801,053	3,801,021	100.00%	14,786	14,785	0.389%	0.389%	0.33	1.29	$4,918.27	11,919	6,348
Lifetime	SCENE75_21+ WITHIN 25 MILES_FRIENDS CONNECTED	GO-KART PHOTO_LARGEST ENTERTAINMENT TEXT	324,610	295,865	91.14%	203	182	0.063%	0.062%	0.36	0.22	$72.18	94	34
Lifetime	SCENE75_21+ WITHIN 25 MILES_FRIENDS CONNECTED	GO-KART PHOTO_ATTRACTION TEXT	350,127	328,596	93.85%	257	246	0.073%	0.075%	0.34	0.25	$87.80	98	68
Lifetime	SCENE75_21+ WITHIN 25 MILES_FRIENDS NOT CONNECTED	GO-KART PHOTO AND LARGEST IN COUNTRY TEXT	1,121,295	816,640	72.83%	648	470	0.058%	0.058%	0.40	0.23	$258.90	260	158
Lifetime	SCENE75_18 TO 20 WITHIN 25 MILES_FRIENDS CONNECTED	SPONSORED STORY	366,634	366,632	100.00%	674	674	0.184%	0.184%	0.24	0.43	$158.63	659	360
Lifetime	SCENE75_21+ WITHIN 50 MILES_FRIENDS CONNECTED	SPONSORED STORY	7,805,269	7,805,210	100.00%	19,271	19,270	0.247%	0.247%	0.29	0.71	$5,564.51	14,397	7,783

$11,477.22 for 15,876 advertising driven page likes = $0.72 per "like"

But many others also saw our logo, saw ad but didn't click, clicked on ad but didn't join, joined our page after seeing in their newsfeed that their friends joined our page... all built brand awareness!

Scene75's Facebook marketing campaign, prior to opening to the public

In taking a closer look at the chart, you will notice that my $11,477.22 in total expenditures yielded 14,539,706 impressions and 15,876 advertising-driven likes to my Facebook page; in other words, my ad appeared nearly 15 million times, with 15,876 people "joining" our page as a direct result of the campaign, equating to an acquisition cost of $0.72 per fan.

What the chart fails to show, however, are all of the indirect benefits the campaign generated for my page, and thus, for my soon-to-open business. In addition to the 15,876 individuals who *joined* the page, there were many unaccounted for who casually saw our logo, saw the ad but did not click on it, clicked on the ad but did not join, or joined our page after seeing in their primary newsfeed that their friends had joined our page. I surmise the indirect benefits may as valuable as the direct, driving down the calculated cost per fan even further.

A prospective fan who saw my ad on the side of the page would not only see that his or her best friend likes Scene75's page (assuming that he or she does, of course) but also that many others whom he or she knows like it as well. As Ron H. posted one month prior to our opening, "What is this place? I've never heard of it, and I have four coworkers that have 'liked' it ... "

Social endorsement becomes such a compelling force, or at the very least a curiosity instigator, when a Facebook ad indicates that Joe (the best friend's name, for illustration's sake), Mary (another friend's name), and two other friends of the prospective fan also like Scene75.

As our fan base grew, it became fairly common for a Scene75 sponsored story to appear on someone's page with an indication that his or her friend liked the page, in addition to nearly *50* other friends. Yes, *50* other friends! This is incredibly potent. And through this power, more and more local fans flocked to Scene75's page. And the more local fans liked the page, the better the odds of having a strong, successful business immediately upon its opening.

In the graph that follows, I share a visual depiction of the explosive growth of Scene75's Facebook page. Although it looks like minimal growth occurred prior to April 14, the time at which I started to invest in Facebook advertisements, the page still grew organically at 100 local fans per day. But as you can see, advertising *clearly* provided tremendous acceleration to this growth.

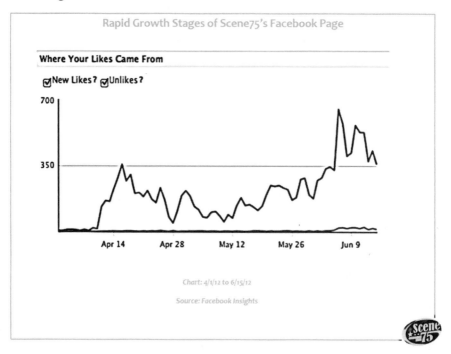

Scene75's daily Facebook fan growth, pre-opening

I hesitated to include this graph in this book because I do not want to convey that advertising on Facebook is the panacea for the problem of creating a successful fan page. It is one influential tool to accelerate what you are already doing. If you fail to produce interesting content, existing fans will be unlikely to share your posts with their friends or to talk about your business at the dinner table. And they most certainly will not turn into highly influential brand advocates! Some fans may even leave your page altogether. The key, therefore, is to bring fans to your page through points of differentiation and to keep them engaged once there — not just for a day and not just for a week, but for the lifetime of your Facebook page. You will see that Facebook marketing requires care, dedication and hard work, but I found that no other use of my marketing time or budget could have produced such meaningful results.

Chapter 9

While our pre-opening fanfare was beyond remarkable, the most important test remained in proving the value of Facebook as a marketing platform. Could the fans on my page translate into actual revenue?

After all, General Motors had just announced in an article titled "GM Says Facebook Ads Don't Pay Off" in the *Wall Street Journal* in May 2012, the same week of Facebook's initial public offering and two months prior to Scene75's opening, that it would stop advertising on Facebook after deciding that its ads on the site had little impact on consumers' car purchases. The GM article raised many questions marketers had been asking worldwide, with the most critical being whether Facebook could directly help companies sell product. But as I quickly learned upon opening Scene75, the answer to this question was a resounding, "Yes!"

People waited in line long before the doors opened each day. We filled every parking space daily within hours of opening, resulting in Facebook posts urging us to expand our 400-plus-car parking lot (which we soon did to accommodate another 70 cars). We reached fire code capacity of 1,300 people every Saturday for months. We set one sales record after another, not only within our own facility but also across the global entertainment industry at large; manufacturers indicated that several of Scene75's attractions were among the busiest of their kind across the world. And I had many guests, some of whom typically refrain from visiting entertainment establishments such as ours, visit simply to meet me, the man behind Scene75's Facebook page.

Left image: Guests waiting in line before the doors opened

Right image: Guests inside Scene75

But I know what you are thinking. Scene75's booming business is not necessarily a direct result of Facebook. After all, Scene75 is a large entertainment center that received coverage in newspapers, other news media, and special publications, in addition to being geographically located just south of a busy I-75, I-70 highway intersection, with clear visibility from the road. Correlation of Facebook activity and the business's success may be evident, but could we prove causation? Not necessarily. So how could the answer be vividly clear to me when many trained marketers, including those from renowned firms, remained unsure about whether Facebook could directly help companies sell their products or services? Because I tested it on many occasions.

The first test was Scene75's opening day. According to all previously released media reports, including that on the front page of the *Dayton Daily News*, Scene75 was set to open on Tuesday, July 3. But given the personal connection I had built with my Facebook fans, I felt that they deserved to be the first ones to experience the entertainment center. So on Monday, July 2, I created and posted an admittedly very poor quality thirty-second video titled "You may ALL find this interesting" (the laughable quality video remains on our Facebook page if you wish to see it). In the video, I pretended that I was opening the door to provide a guided tour, but in a surprise announcement, I shared that Scene75 was officially open to the public. Facebook fans, and Facebook fans alone, were the first to know that we were open for business that day!

Within minutes, my fans went wild. They loved the shocking video, regardless of the footage quality. As Laurie C. posted, "GREAT way to announce it! You all are amazing!" Or as Lake V. posted, "Jonah … u are ate up bud … u should go into commercial advertising ... seriously ... "

They posted congratulatory messages, many of which were directed to me personally; they felt like they knew me, given that I had taken them along on the journey with me.

As Susan E. posted, "Congratulations, Jonah. I am sure it feels surreal to finally open your doors to everyone. Best wishes to your success; may all your hard work bring you only the best!" Or as Donna R. expressed, "Holy cow … way to go Jonah. Great news!!!"

They posted messages of sheer enthusiasm. Lisa R. shared, "So happy to hear that you're open. I will pass the word to everyone I know!!! Yay!!!" Or as Shane J. expressed, "OMG, I LOVE YOU *kisses*."

But most important, they posted messages indicating that they would be visiting that same evening:

Sandy M.: "We'll be there in about an hour for dinner! Yay!!!"

Andrew A.: "OMG! I now have something to do this evening!!!"

43

Michael R.: "Oh awesome and I just got off early!!!"

Kami S.: "I'm coming! Yayyyyyyyyyy."

Adam S.: "What???????? I am coming tonight right after work!!! Hope you guys are open around 11."

Timothy W.: "As soon as I get off work and my wife does, I'm gonna try to get her to come over there with me today. Trying to track her down right now! Can't wait to see it!"

This particular video post generated 705 likes, 144 shares, and 111 comments. And it filled the parking lot within hours, and with it, our cash drawers.

But our opening date was only the first of many experiments that would illustrate the effectiveness of Facebook's ability to create sales. Perhaps the most salient example, and the one that would ultimately lead me to capture the attention and respect of Facebook itself, was Halloween 2012. This is what happened.

At 9:35 a.m. on October 30, 2012, the morning before Halloween yet the day of local Trick or Treat, Nick A. posted the following to our Facebook page:

"What do you think about spreading out several employees around Scene75 with candy and letting the kids have an indoor Beggars' Night there, since this weather is simply MISERABLE. Especially for the little ones who deserve to Trick or Treat but don't deserve to be in this weather?"

In truth, I had brainstormed an idea similar to Nick's a few weeks prior, but I had worried that its execution would lead to safety risks given the likelihood of guests wearing masks, bringing toy weapons, and wearing capes on rides. But the weather was *so* wretched that morning, complete with heavy wind, sleet and snow, that his comment provoked further interest from fellow Facebook fans:

Stacey A.: "Like!"

Stafanie J.: "I would even be willing to bring the candy I bought to hand out and donate it to you all to give out! Or even stand there and hand it out myself."

Shelli N.: "I agree with that entirely; the kids will be disappointed or if not enough time tonight do it tomorrow night double treat for some kids. My 4 year old grandson won't be here til tomorrow night and he will be so disappointed ... "

Traci C.: "It's my son's first Halloween, and I'm sad he might miss it."

Jessica F.: "We were gonna do a family thing in tonight but that's a really great idea for even the older kids; my son is 8 and sad if he isn't going anywhere."

As additional comments began to trickle in supporting the idea (Nick's post would ultimately receive 76 likes and 64 comments in a relatively short period of time), I decided that I could not resist any longer. Scene75, though an entertainment center by design, was first and foremost a community center. And as the CEO of a community center, it was my duty to make Scene75 available to the community in a time of perceived need. So at 11:48 a.m., two hours after Nick's initial post, I decided to push ahead and post the following announcement to our page:

YOU ASKED, WE LISTENED.

WEATHER STINKS SO LET'S INDOOR TRICK OR TREAT...

SCENE75 STYLE

CANDY AT EVERY ATTRACTION. 6 TO 8 P.M. TONIGHT!

STAY WARM. BE SAFE.

Scene75's Facebook post on October 30, 2012

Within minutes of my post, supportive comments began to hit our page:

Kelli B. at 11:49 a.m.: "I almost called yesterday and asked if you were doing anything. I am so excited. Thank you for stepping up for the community."

Jessica A. at 11:50 a.m.: "Thank you, thank you, thank you! My three year old was devastated we weren't going to be able to go out in the cold!"

Lindsay R. at 11:57 a.m.: "Kids should enjoy getting candy, not get frostbite from getting candy!! So blessed a place like Scene75 would do that!!"

Chelsie L. at 12:19 p.m.: "Way to be a business that is supportive of the community! I think this is truly great."

Sarah A. at 12:35 p.m.: "I absolutely love that a suggestion was present to you and you made it happen immediately! Way to be a supportive business in the community! I am so glad Scene75 decided to call Dayton home!"

Candice H. at 12:54 p.m.: "You guys are a lifesaver. It's going to be super cold and have been fighting with myself all morning on whether or not to take my daughter out tonight. Thanks for saving the day."

It was now nearly 1 p.m., leaving only five hours until the first of hopefully many trick-or-treaters would be at our door. I had to act quickly if we were to be ready for the evening. As I began to lay out the strategy in my office, my father, who worked alongside me, wondered what I was doing. I told him that I was preparing for the crowd that I expected that evening. I explained that if Facebook was any indication of the imminent turnout, we would be busy (my initial post generated 495 likes and 200 shares after it ran its course). But my dad, who openly admits that he does not understand the Internet (and is still to this day the only person I know without an e-mail address), felt that I would not be able to attract even 50 people in costume the entire night, given the short notice, and that, frankly, I was crazy for even trying. But as I mentioned in the opening of this book, an entrepreneur is indeed just that.

So I pushed ahead. I notified teammates of the plan for the evening while encouraging them to arrive in costume. I drove around town like a madman picking up Halloween decorations at any store where I could find last-minute inventory. I developed a quick plan for a costume contest. I helped the team set up the newly purchased Halloween décor. I organized hundreds of pounds of candy typically reserved for arcade prizes, reclassifying it as free trick-or-treat candy. And I responded to Facebook posts on my smartphone to answer questions as they poured in, while encouraging fans to spread the word. And I did all of this while grinning, knowing that for once I had a chance to prove my dad wrong!

As 6 p.m. rolled around, the moment of truth was upon my team. Within five minutes of what would ultimately become a three-hour trick-or-treat extravaganza, we had more than 50 people in costume. Within thirty minutes, we had a building full of trick-or-treaters and a line out the door ... a line that would continue for hours.

Halloween 2012 at Scene75 Entertainment Center

That evening, I posted the following text and picture to our page, a post that remains one of the most popular posts in our brief history, having received 1,979 likes, 132 comments, and 33 platform shares:

"AMAZING NIGHT. Today we proved the power of a community. At nearly 1 p.m. today we decided to announce we would be hosting an indoor trick-or-treating event given the weather conditions. Only 5 hours later, with word spreading by Facebook, TV [a television broadcaster did visit a few hours into the event, but in truth, her timing was too late for the fantastic turnout to be attributable to her report], and word of mouth, we packed Scene75 and filled the parking lot for hours, with a line out the door as pictured. We estimate that we handed out 350+ pounds of candy [which I grossly underestimated by nearly 500 pounds] and saw more than 2,000 trick or treaters throughout the evening. Glad we could give the children in our community a Halloween to remember. Thanks for the support. Our Scene75 family enjoyed doing this for the community."

Halloween 2012 at Scene75 Entertainment Center

(Maximum occupancy within facility forced guests to wait in line outside)

The following day, I created yet another post that would draw significant fanfare, this one to the tune of 1,327 likes and 62 comments:

"ALRIGHT, I HAVE TO POST THIS. SORRY DAD! Despite being one of my all-time biggest supporters, he doubted that last night would be a success with only 5 hours to announce, prepare and host. He told me that I would surprise him if we had 50 people show up in costume. I tried to make a wager with him, but I guess he has learned to not bet against me – I hate to lose! We had 50 in costume within 5 minutes of our 3 hour trick or treat event. At that point, my grin was huge, and I made sure to find him to count those in costumes. He then told me 'If you can fill the parking lot tonight, you deserve a prize'. A thousand plus costumes later, I hope he is putting that prize together now. Love ya, Dad."

Responsive comments from fans illustrated the amazing goodwill built from this last-minute event:

Teresa S.: "Think it's great you've came to our town and have opened your arms to our families! Welcome to the neighborhood! Wish more businesses would quit worrying about how much money they can make off of us and instead be a good steward to the town! Thanks Scene75!"

Dee Dee M.: "Trick or treating along with laser tag and a few arcade games made for an epic Halloween! I was looking for a place to take my daughter and there were many posts on other company's Facebook pages, including the malls, and no one stepped up but you! Thanks Scene75!"

Jan H.: "Jonah, you must have made your dad very proud and a big prize is well deserved. We got there at 6:15; you would have never known it was a last minute event; there was nowhere to park in your lot. What you put together in a matter of 5 hours for the community was just amazing … a huge thanks for a job well done!"

Nick M.: "I'm still impressed that you were able to put this together so fast. Even with only a few hours notice the turnout was awesome! I saw a lot of happy children tonight! Once again thank you very much!"

Bobbisue H.: "I finally figured out why we went from 200 trick or treaters to a mere 20 this year … SCENE75!! We live nearby and I'm starting to think all of our neighborhood kids headed over to your place last night! That's okay … we'll probably do that with the kids next year! ;) Thank you for being such a great destination for entertainment right here at home! We love you! See you on the 10th for my daughter's 6th birthday!"

Kelly K.: "I am very thankful you guys put something together for this area! It was a horrible night for trick or treat and knowing you had an excellent place and event going as an indoor alternative was AWESOME!! Thank you for stepping up and being a community wide team player."

Brandon H.: "Very, very, cool. Just hope you had runners for candy if anyone ran out. Support a great local establishment, Dayton!"

Goodwill of this nature simply cannot be purchased, and I know of very few, if any, marketing media today in which I could have created such an overwhelming response in such a short period of time. Halloween 2012 proved to be our heaviest day of traffic in the brief history of our establishment. And it was through Facebook that within a matter of hours, the idea was generated, the word was spread, the facility was filled, revenue was generated, and unbelievable goodwill for my business was established. I undeniably built a brand that day … and I did it through Facebook.

Chapter 10

In addition to providing a platform to generate sales, Facebook proved invaluable as a customer service tool on a near daily basis.

I often tell my teammates that when a guest is unhappy, I would much prefer to receive a complaint from that guest than to have never known about it. When dining out, my parents will often stay quiet when they face an issue with their meals, only to never return to that establishment. From a business owner's perspective, this is a nightmare — the guest leaves without informing management, only to never return, and in the process, he or she may tell a dozen friends to refrain from visiting that particular establishment. I found that Facebook served as a non-intimidating outlet for guests to comfortably express their frustrations — guests who, like my parents, may have never complained in person. Furthermore, the complaints often were immediate, allowing for timely attention.

I can recall several instances when a guest voiced a concern on Facebook, and I responded while he or she was still in the facility! Not only did my response ease the concern, but the immediate attention to the issue shocked him or her. In turn, I built a fan out of someone who otherwise may have left and never returned to Scene75. Here is one of my favorite such examples made possible through Facebook. Amber A. visited one month after we opened. While she was still in the facility (which I didn't know at the time), Amber posted the following:

"Save time with go-karts. Get the next group in the karts while the current race is finishing. Wait time is ridiculous here!"

I saw this message while sitting at an office computer, and I immediately responded:

"Hi Amber. After reading your comment, I went back to the racetrack to talk to the team. They typically load the next group while the current group is on the track, but tonight some of the cars were having difficulty keeping their full charge given the [particularly heavy] use of last night and today. We are looking into some battery options to resolve this problem, but the team decided to not load the other group tonight as letting a group into the cars would limit the charging capabilities with people continually pressing on the pedals. Sorry for the wait; we will get there; still tweaking as we go."

Within minutes, Amber responded: "I must admit. I am highly impressed with the timely manner in which you addressed this issue. I was actually standing in line [at the go-karts] when you came to check. It's good to see that your patrons and their opinions matter."

To which I followed: "Thank you Amber, we care immensely about our guests and this facility. We are learning each day and finding out the limitations of the equipment. Working on solutions … "

Without Facebook, I do not know that this guest would have expressed her concerns, and thus, I may never have had the chance to rectify the problem. But I did. And in the process, I created a supportive fan.

Facebook also proved helpful in providing a platform for guests to suggest ideas for our development or to guide us where they noticed weaknesses. Admittedly, most ideas were left as nothing more than ideas, but we did implement quite a few.

Lana H. explained one month after opening, "Took my grandkids there last weekend. They weren't old enough to do almost everything. I wish you would add a section with games for the younger kids, like 3, 4 and 5 years old … " We added additional arcade games for our youngest visitors later that month.

Some suggestions were far more basic, so basic that if a teammate had been told the suggestion in passing, he or she may not have thought to mention it to me. But as I quickly learned upon opening, even such basics are important.

Tina L. posted two weeks after opening: "Stopped by last night and had a really good time. May I make a suggestion? Could you put hooks under the bar for our purses? It's a huge pain to have to keep my purse on my lap or sit it on the bar next to my drink. Otherwise, we had a perfect time. Keep up the great work!" While such details are trivial to most guests, the suggestion was simple enough to implement. And if it impacted even one person's experience, I wanted to address it. Hooks were installed underneath the bar that week.

Sometimes fans would simply guide us about where additional staff training was needed. As Brian C. shared:

"Went back for a return visit this past Saturday and checked out the 3D/4D attraction. While we had fun on the ride, the 3D portion seemed a bit off for the 4 of us. Everything was very distorted with the glasses on, we all had to close one eye for everything to line up and look normal and did this for pretty much the extent of the ride.

Once I was in a 3D movie and the same thing happened, everyone in the theater complained and they did something to fix it, not quite sure what. Thought I'd pass it along to you though."

If my team and I were to achieve our mission of being not only the largest indoor entertainment center in the country but also the best, we needed to fine-tune the details. And often, it was only through Facebook that I learned what required tweaking.

Chapter 11

Given the impact of Facebook on my business, the rapid success of Scene75, my passion for helping others, and a desire to make our entertainment center a true community pillar, I dedicated several hours each week to helping other small-business owners in my geographic area better understand and implement Facebook marketing. I started small, with one-on-one pro-bono coaching. Eventually, I invited fans to attend a live seminar at Scene75, where I shared my journey — which I detail in this book — to build a strong, vibrant Facebook page in a short period of time. I initially intended to host only one such seminar, but after significant fanfare on Facebook from those who attended and many requests from those who were unable to attend the first seminar, I ultimately hosted several more, with as many as 60 business owners and organization leaders attending a single session.

Hosting a Facebook marketing seminar at Scene75 Entertainment Center

During each presentation, I hosted a question and answer session. Through several of the audience's questions, I learned that Facebook, to many attendees, was a mysterious platform; they knew that their business should be on Facebook, but they were unsure how to develop a meaningful presence. I gained valuable insight from their thoughts — so much so that I shared key takeaways with my contacts at Facebook, several of whom had started to follow our page long before we opened.

Eager to learn more about the insights offered in my presentations, Facebook sent Katy Castleberry, a company representative, to attend one of the presentations. (I was informed that this was the first time a Facebook employee had ever attended an external presentation by a small business about Facebook marketing.)

Katy and I

After listening to my presentation, Katy returned to Facebook headquarters, where I'm told my story began to spread among her teammates. Over the following few months, I shared frequent updates with my now personal contacts at Facebook, ultimately leading to one of the most touching honors of my life. I was invited to represent more than 15 million small business pages as a speaker at Facebook's Annual Global Sales Meeting in May 2013.

With nervous energy miraculously wrapped in a sense of calm collectedness, I delivered a 15-minute presentation to more than 1,300 Facebook employees. I shared the story within this book, in addition to my thoughts about how Facebook could better help small businesses around the world, the group I was essentially there to represent. As I stood on stage, teleprompters surrounded me with cues from my prepared presentation. But the story was my own. I had lived the journey the last several years, and I knew the story so well that I spoke entirely from within, sharing the deepest truths and emotions I knew. As with the Scene75 Facebook page, my words were greeted with passionate enthusiasm, leading to many of the supportive comments from Facebook employees listed at the beginning of this book.

The day following my presentation, as I sat at a coffee shop in California waiting for my flight back to Ohio, I shared my experience and the following image on Scene75's Facebook page:

"Without question, this has been one of the most fascinating times of my life. Nearly two months ago, Facebook leadership asked me to represent more than 15 million small businesses at its global sales meeting in California. On Thursday morning, I did just that by sharing my personal journey and that of Scene75 with 1,300 Facebook employees. It was an incredible experience that can best be described as surreal. I delivered a 15-minute presentation, with what must have been a 50-foot wide PowerPoint screen behind me, to arguably the most influential company in the world today. Though most in the room had never met me nor heard of Scene75, as I shared my story it quickly became clear to me that I was more than a page to them. I was a person with whom my story resonated at a personal level, much as it did with many of you. There were moments of applause, moments of tears, and moments of human connectivity. In the same light as my not being a page to them, they were no longer the virtual world to me; they were caring, kind-hearted people who were genuinely inspired by the footprints of my journey — particularly so given that they gave me the "virtual ground" to walk on. As I sit at a coffee shop in California typing this, I am reminded as to how grateful I am for all of you, our fans. You made it possible. You are the reason Scene75 exists. You are the reason we have been successful (and will remain the reason for our success going forward). You are the reason Facebook had an interest in our story. You are the reason Facebook asked me to stand before a crowd of 1,300 employees to represent millions of businesses at the conference. And you are the reason I now have a memory that I will truly cherish forever. Thank you for building this dream with me. It has been, and will always be, one of the highlights of my life." *May 10, 2013 – Scene75 – 675 likes, 80 comments and 27 shares*

Dan Levy, director of small business, introduces me to the team at Facebook

A few months after the Facebook presentation in San Francisco, Scene75's efforts were again recognized at an international level, this time at the 2013 International Association of Amusement Parks and Attractions expo in Orlando, Florida. IAAPA, the largest international association of amusement facilities in the world, nominated Scene75 for several awards, including best public relations program in the entertainment industry. With my mom and dad among the thousands of attendees, Scene75 won the Brass Ring Award for Marketing Excellence, which recognizes the best within the entertainment industry. My dad, holding back tears of happiness, joined me onstage to accept the award.

Dad and I accept the Brass Ring Award from an IAAPA representative

Within days of our winning the award, my dad, along with my Facebook fans, reminded me of a post created one year earlier, in May 2012, nearly two months before Scene75 officially opened. I had written that I wanted to win an award that would recognize Scene75 and its community of supporters as among the best in the industry:

"I am often asked when I find time to sleep. Truth is, I find the time (well, at least enough time to survive) — but I rarely CAN sleep. Here's why: 1) I am so passionate about Scene75 that a part of me feels like I'm missing out on something when I'm not engaged 2) Scene75, along with the Chaos Room in Centerville and Putters Par-adise in Englewood, have been my life the last three years, and well, I have grown accustomed to making certain sacrifices during this time period; of my extended list of sacrifices, sleep is actually one of the easier ones on that list—more on this to come perhaps at a later date depending on what you, our fans, actually want to know about the journey of the makings of Scene75; however, I can tell you that given the sacrifices made, this would have to be an amazing center to justify them 3) My list of things to do seems to get longer each day no matter how many items I cross off with my Sharpie 4) I refuse to settle for less than my best; seeing your support encourages me to elevate my game to an even higher playing field, and I genuinely thank you for that 5) My friends, family, partners and I have so much skin in the game and a hardened belief in me that I simply don't want to let anyone down—and I won't 6) I am determined to make Scene75 something Dayton will be proud of now and for years to come 7) I want this to be the BEST entertainment center in the country, and I am out to win an award to back that up 8) I don't want to let you all down— this place WILL be great!" *May 31, 2012 – Scene75 – 207 likes and 37 comments*

As a result of our successes, the mayor honored Scene75 with a proclamation marking December 18 as Scene75 Day, *Ohio Magazine* named Scene75 the best place for family fun in its 2014 Best of Ohio issue, and Facebook subsequently asked me to serve on its inaugural Small and Medium Business Council. I joined eleven other businesses to serve a one-year term, advising Facebook on the development of its tools.

I suppose sometimes dreams do come true.

Chapter 12

The world is undoubtedly a competitive, crowded marketplace. As a small-business owner, it is almost imperative to identify a niche to differentiate yourself from the competition. Facebook allowed me to carve the niche I needed to create a successful business.

I surmise that those struggling to see the power of Facebook's potential, such as those in the GM article previously referenced, fail to see the platform for what it represents — a forum of two-way communication where one can share information at such an emotional level that it can captivate fans and make them genuinely *want* to provide support. I made Scene75's Facebook page personal. I positioned it to tug at the hearts of my readers. I created engaging content that only I could reveal, content that my readers devoured. I listened to what they wanted ... and I delivered. I shared my truths, and both goodwill and sales subsequently followed.

I conclude with a *very* personal note that I shared with my Facebook fans on July 23, 2012, three weeks after we opened, to the tune of 491 likes and 37 comments. It is a note that summarizes the most gratifying aspect of my journey, and if it were not for Facebook, I might never have received it:

"Wow. Look what my parents gave me this weekend. The note was on the back of the framed article. Thank you for helping me shape the dream."

Gift received from my parents three weeks after Scene75 opened

Appendix: Fun Additional Posts, Ordered by Date of Post

Pre-Opening

"Heard about you guys all the way in Texas! Sounds like a great place. We are visiting Ohio in the summer and I just looked it up and we will only be 37 miles away from your location. I found out what we are doing!!" *January 28, 2012 – Denise W.*

"Our laser tag second level play structure installers just arrived. They have constructed arenas all over the country. First comment they made to us: 'My goodness! We have never seen such a large laser tag arena.' Welcome to Scene75 fellas." *May 7, 2012 – Scene75 – 134 likes, 10 comments*

"Yep, that's a six foot tall man standing next to it ..." *May 11, 2012 – Scene75 – 187 likes, 32 comments and 21 shares.*

"Fun story. I had my Scene75 hoodie on when I took a break for dinner last night; the entire host staff swarmed around me for all of the latest Scene75 updates. This morning I held the door for a lady and her family as I was leaving in my Scene75 apparel — she walked in and overheard her telling her family how excited she is about our facility. This afternoon at the gas station a gentlemen behind me noticed the Scene75 logo on my shirt as I was pumping gas and asked me when we would be opening. THIS IS TRULY AMAZING. The enthusiasm is invigorating. Thank you!" *May 19, 2012 – Scene75 – 206 likes and 33 comments*

"My man Alex was so excited to see 3 courts of volleyball sand that he couldn't control his enthusiasm! Sand angel signals the start of summer!?!?!" *May 24, 2012 – Scene75 – 135 likes and 15 comments*

"Per a post yesterday, I wanted to share a very kind e-mail I received with Laura's permission to share. Exciting times here. 'Hi Jonah. I follow Scene75 on Facebook and as a marketing/PR pro, I just have to say that you are one of the best businesses on FB that I have come across. I love how you take us day by day through what is happening and the business isn't even opened yet. So many times, we teach business owners to start their FB page when they are open for business, but you have shown me a completely different way to promote a business through FB. We all feel like we know you, can't wait to see your sister's artwork [which I promised would be hanging on several interior walls], want to meet your uncle [a subject of several fan favorite posts], search for that hamburger on the golf hole [a prop on our mini-golf course] and more than anything, we know the face behind this huge business that is coming to Dayton. We feel like we know you and trust you as a business owner — THAT is what Facebook for businesses is supposed to be about. I advise over 700 franchises in the senior home care industry on social media (we are the second largest in-home care company in the world based here in Dayton) ... and I'd love to use you as an example on how to connect to your community through FB. I'd like to share some of your posts and show them how you built this excitement with personal stories, things happening, etc. as you worked to open the business. Thanks so much for opening up your world, sharing your adventure, and taking us on your journey as you open Scene 75. I know it is going to do so much for our community and you have stirred up so much excitement! Thanks!'" *June 6, 2012 – Scene75 – 296 likes and 29 comments*

"Truly enjoying my team. I feel like I'm in my college dorm again — people staying up late to work, hang out and get to know one another all while on a mission to pass! Ok, maybe to get straight A's ... but still ... haha. Loving the hard work everyone is putting in to see this place come together sooner rather than later." *June 6, 2012 – Scene75 – 83 likes and 18 comments*

"Tonight I share a rather lengthy, personal anecdote. As some of you may have read from researching my background (LOL ... read that a few of you have done that in a prior comment stream ... STALKERS ... just kidding ... you are the best ... feel free to research away), I graduated in 2009 from an MBA program. Shortly after graduation, I mentioned to a professor my desire to leave an investment banking offer on the table and instead take a giant leap of faith to create entertainment concepts in my hometown. He challenged me in a number of regards, but always welcomed my thoughts, calls and e-mails—and took a true interest in what I set out to do. On one specific phone call from Dayton two+ years ago, I introduced my professor to my father. They chatted for a little while before we all dug deep into the heart of the matter—Putters Par-adise, Chaos Room, and a project that seemed SO distant that it was hardly worth a mention—Scene75. Well, just yesterday, my father, without my knowing, e-mailed a letter to my professor after an extended absence of communication to inform him that Scene75 would soon become a reality. Along with the letter, he included an outline I wrote the other night for a book I'd love to one day find the time to write (perhaps while sitting in that seemingly elusive hammock). Well, my professor supposedly responded today with shared enthusiasm and indicated that he personally can't wait to read the book ... It's been a wild journey my friends ... it truly has been wild. The twists, the turns, the reversals, and quite frankly, the all too many potholes, have discouraged me and the team time and time again from carrying on. So what, you may wonder, kept me going? Honestly? FEAR and a love for my family. I knew what I sacrificed to begin this journey (paychecks, free time, romantic love, etc.), and for me, stopping halfway was simply not an option. I realized I'd rather fail trying to do something I loved for a purpose I loved than to never have tried at all. Truth is, if it weren't for you all, I'd be absolutely terrified of the weeks ahead and my mind would be racing with questions—would people come, would people enjoy, can this work in Dayton, etc. Now, I'm more terrified that I won't be able to greet each and every one of you in person because so many of you will be here in full force! Thank you, thank you, thank you! I hardly sleep now, but I can say with almost certainty that I would sleep far less if I didn't have you to lean on." *June 6, 2012 – Scene75 – 285 likes and 86 comments*

"I would just like to congratulate you on the outstanding success of this business. So much support and so much success before you even open the doors! I really enjoy your daily posts about the progress and am humbled by your personal notes. It's nice to know the face behind the business and it feels like we all already know you. I haven't met a person yet who isn't as excited as I am for opening day, whenever that may be. What a great development for the Dayton area. Can't wait to come have a day/night of fun and be close enough to walk to home. A big congrats for everything you are accomplishing and a big thank you for the same!" *June 7, 2012 – Amy A.*

"Let me say this. I'm pretty much exhausted — totally spent. But work remains. I just left Scene75 to stop by the office; going to grab a late bite to eat before catching up on the additional 70 e-mails waiting in my inbox. But before I do this, I just want to say thank you. While I was away from Facebook, I received dozens of text messages from my friends at the Racing Place counting up from 11,983 [fans] to 12,000 that read as follows: "9, 8, 7, 5, You have to post something!, 3, 1, POST, 12,000!" Wow! And just a minute ago, we overtook what I know to be the largest fan base of any non-chain entertainment center in the country — at least of all of those I have ever encountered or researched ... which is quite a few. Despite all of this, the journey is now at a new beginning. Tomorrow I look forward to meeting, working with, and hopefully inspiring many of my newest teammates to deliver their personal best such that we can make Scene75 the place it NEEDS to become. Having struggled to get to this point over a three year time period, everything seems surreal. But then I realize how tired I am and quickly recognize that yep, this is all actually happening! And I couldn't be more thrilled. Good night my friends. Thank you for supporting me on this mission, for encouraging others to join the adventure, and for embracing all that Scene75 is to become. Truly amazing. 12,097 [fans]. And the doors have yet to open ... " *June 7, 2012 – Scene75 – 211 likes and 40 comments*

"Three days of training and we have only just begun to have fun! Won't my grandkids think I'm the cool grandma to be working in such a rockin' place — the word was "hip" in my day! I am still pinching myself to see if it's true that I am in on the building of the greatest fun place ... leave troubles and stress at the door and get an endorphin infusion! Our training team is working so hard and not only are they smart, but they are personable ... an amazing experience that I'm THRILLED to join! Props to our trainers! I can't say enough good about them ... " *June 10, 2012 – Jackie W.*

"I am often asked what it is that I have enjoyed most about this journey. I suppose there are three elements. 1) I love the design element; I truly enjoyed taking an empty warehouse building and layout out the entire facility 2) I love interacting with each of you here on Facebook; I feel like I have developed a personal connection with many of you, even though most of you I have yet to meet in person 3) I love the team element; I love teaching, sharing, learning, and being a part of something where I am an equal to my teammates — our success rests in their hands; I can only do so much as an individual, but as a team, we can achieve greatness." *June 10, 2012 – Scene75 – 208 likes and 40 comments*

"I am sitting down on my couch for what feels like the first time in months. In doing so, I wanted to share some feedback stemming from our recent orientation session, all in hope of giving you a 'behind the Scene' look into what we are doing here. I received permission to share. Thank you! 'Jonah I just wanted to personally thank you for allowing me to be a part of your team. The way that you & the rest of your team treat all of us new employees coming into this is incredible to me. You have all welcomed us with open arms & treated us as equals & I cannot tell you how nice it is to work for a company who treats their employees like family. I like what I do at my other job but the way that place is managed leaves a lot to be desired. You guys all make me want to be better myself. I just want you to know that what you are doing definitely does not go unnoticed. I was excited about Scene75 before I met you and your team but now that I have met you guys & I see how you work & why you are doing what you are doing here in the Dayton area, I am even more excited & have absolutely no doubt that this business is going to be successful. So thank you to you & your whole team for creating a place that I love to work already. I promise you that I will always give you & this company 100% & I cannot wait for opening day.' It means a lot to me to see this type of feeling in my new teammates. Thank you! Excited to continue the journey and learn more about each and every one of them ... " *June 11, 2012 – Scene75 – 114 likes and 13 comments*

"I cannot express just how excited I am to start working! Can't wait till we open!" *June 12, 2012 – Rebecca R.*

"Pull up a stool. Tell me your story. I will be the worst bartender we have, but I look forward to setting up behind the bar one night to chat it up with you … " *June 13, 2012 – Scene75 – 419 likes and 56 comments*

"20,000 fans! Soon our glasses will be full. Thanks for joining us on this journey. Can't wait to meet you all!" *June 27, 2012 – Scene75 – 378 likes and 17 comments*

"I tried a burger today fresh off the grill of the newly installed and inspected kitchen. We are all in for a treat! The service was outstanding as well—the personal attention … incredible. ;) " *June 28, 2012 – Scene75 – 240 likes and 40 comments*

Opening Date, July 2, 2012

"I go to bed so inspired tonight. Here's why. 1) My team is so passionate about getting this right and helping me fulfill a dream. It's a beautiful thing to experience. Truly is something unique to see a hundred people eager to give something their all. I am so proud of them for caring about this facility and our guests as much as I do. 2) Our community is so supportive. I love meeting each of you. I feel so fortunate merely to sense the appreciation you have for this facility. Truly inspiring to me. Thank you." *July 4, 2012 – Scene75 – 344 likes and 53 comments*

"Don't let the line fool you. It really wasn't that bad of a wait. I've been there 3 days this week. It's addicting." *July 6, 2012 – Rhoda O.*

"I went to Scene75 last night and really enjoyed it; I could not believe everything you guys had ... also I was playing one of the games and when I slid my card the coins did not come out for me to play; as I was standing there an older gentleman that works there came over asked me what the problem was. Not only did he find me someone to put more coins into the machine but he also pulled out his wallet and handed me a dollar ... that's what I call GREAT CUSTOMER SERVICE!" *July 7, 2012 – Johnny O.*

"Wow. Where do I begin. Three years ago I started an all-in, all of my chips are on the table, journey in hope of one day seeing an entertainment facility of grand proportions within an empty warehouse building at 6196 Poe Avenue. Tonight, as I reflect upon our first full week of operations at Scene75, I can't help but ask myself, "did this really just happen?" You see, the transition from years of design and planning with a 1% probability of actually seeing Scene75 come to life, to hey, we are now open, took one single day. That's it. And my life as it relates to Scene75, and perhaps beyond, has changed entirely since Monday — I went from planning, designing, drawing, evaluating, rethinking, recreating, and dreaming to implementing, reflecting, reworking, assessing, fixing and greeting. Having met many of you this week, I am delighted to have been able to share my dream and vision with you. I hope you will continue to support us with the fervor you demonstrated this week; it has been a long time since I have witnessed so many smiles within a single setting. It is truly remarkable to see your reactions. Thank you! I'd also like to thank my team. They have been incredible. Though we all worked long, hard hours this week, each member returned to Scene75 with a smile on his or her face and ready to do it all again. I love the passion they have for this facility, their work, and for serving you. I feel very fortunate to have them as my colleagues. Thank you all. Goodnight. See you tomorrow. 3 p.m. to 10 p.m. Monday – Thursday this week." *July 8, 2012 – Scene75 – 581 likes and 71 comments*

"GOOD TIMES! It's coming along great Jonah, we were there tonight and had a blast. I can't imagine how hard it must be to do something at this level with no blueprint. As you've said all along you're gonna make mistakes in this journey, but you are

proactive in making it the best experience for everyone … we're looking forward to coming back out and enjoying more of Scene75 in the next few weeks, heck we still have a ton of money on our cards after going all out! Congrats to a great opening Jonah. We know Scene75 will be a staple for fun in the Dayton community for a long, long time!" *July 8, 2012 – Nick S.*

"Ok!! I read about ur place for 2 hrs last nite!! Read All the Good and Bad comments! Went 2day, w my 7 yr old son, n 67 yr old friend!! All i have 2 say is ..... We had a Freakin Blast!! I have nothing but Rave Reviews!! Ur staff is Fabulous! They were above n beyond helpful!! I dont even like games, but i Can Not wait 2 go back!! U have bout evrything anyone cd possibly want! And, 4 the ppl saying its expensive, its Free to get in ppl! U choose what u wanna spend! 3 of us were there for 4 hrs, spent 100 bux! ... Only thing i cant wait 4 is the 2seater go carts! My son wd luv those! Ur Bumper Cars r so cool! Ive never seen ones that spin 2 music b4!! Btw, i looked 4 u, Jonah, cause i wanted 2 meet u, n thank u, but maybe next time ill find u!! Its Incredible that 1 person cd do all this!! WTG!! We Will B Back later this wk!! N, anyone worried bout long lines gettin in, we got there @ 2:40, n were 1st in line!! Luuuuuved it!" *July 9, 2012 – Ginger F.*

"Thank you Jonah, and your staff for being so sweet and kind to my pageant girl, in the red sparkle dress, Athena today ... she loves your establishment, and your kindness means a lot!! Some of the staff wished her luck and gave her high fives, it's good to have such a huge place, but still feel like you are cared for ... two thumbs up as always!!" *July 10, 2012 – Angela D.*

"Jonah, do we need to make a reservation if we are having a HUGE group coming for a birthday party? It is adults." *July 11, 2012 – Cheryl B.*

"I value all feedback here, truly. It's a great forum to help us refine our processes after only our first 1.5 weeks of operations. Our team reads everything. We are a passionate team, with many of us working from pre-open to post-close, to try to deliver a great experience 7 days a week. The downside of having such a public forum, however, is that human nature is such that those FEW people who received a quality of service less than what we strive for are more likely to voice their opinions than those who have an absolute blast of a time, think this place is an incredible facility, value having an establishment of this nature in what many consider a relatively uneventful city, and appreciate the passion, enthusiasm, care and hard work of each of our team members. We are seeing THOUSANDS of people smile from ear to ear and have an AMAZING time each and every day! My team and I hear SO many positive comments in the facility — this is the best thing to happen to Dayton, the value here is incredible with an opportunity to spend an hour or two here for less than $10, this place trumps any other entertainment facility we have ever been to, your team is AWESOME and so passionate about helping you see your dream unfold, etc. I am grateful for the team in place, those who support us vocally in person and here on Facebook, and the entire community for coming out to support us. The response from each of you in coming to visit us with such fervor that we have HAD to implement certain policies to keep safety at the forefront of this establishment is amazing. My partners, even those who believed in me and my vision, never anticipated that we would see the crowds we are seeing. Thank you from the bottom of my heart for helping me prove my thesis. For those who have yet to visit us, don't let the few negative comments keep you from visiting. Keep in mind that for each negative post, there are probably 50 times that number with amazing experiences who simply haven't posted! Can't wait to see you all today! Noon to 8 p.m.!" *July 15, 2012 – Scene75 – 234 likes and 132 comments*

"I thought I would share some of my favorite highlights of this adventure from the past 2 weeks: Meeting Kathleen (our avid Facebooker who makes me blush—she always follows up her comments with some mention of how cute I am!), my dad walking around the facility while passing out sticky men toys from the redemption center to every guest he met, seeing the dedication of my team to this facility and to our guests (I practically have to force people to take days off because they like working here so much!), having a guest stop me, introduce herself to me, hug me, and take a picture with me, seeing smiles on faces everywhere I turn, meeting a guest who has already visited our facility 7 times, hearing a story of one of our guests who has lost an inch on his waistline (no joke) from playing 5 games of laser tag a day upon each visit (he has been here 5 times), and hearing such positive feedback in person and on Facebook. Thank you all for helping support this dream and for those who have helped us continually improve from day 1 of opening. You all amaze me. The adventure has only begun." *July 16, 2012 – Scene75 – 306 likes and 53 comments*

 "Our lost and found collection is sadly growing. This lovely ensemble is a white, sequin hooded sweatshirt. It belongs to a little girl whose mother was so worried that she lost it forever—it was her absolute favorite! We

found it near the go-karts. Mother of girl ... if you are reading this ... it is here safe for pick up courtesy of kind Melissa at the snack bar. Message us!" [The mother responded to claim the sweatshirt, and another guest asked if we had found his child's missing shoe ... which we did!) *July 20, 2012 – Scene75 – 141 likes, 26 comments and 12 shares*

"Over the last three years, I often questioned if I made the right decision to move back to Ohio. After 3 weeks of seeing smiling faces at Scene75, I think I may finally have an answer ... " *July 24, 2012 – Scene75 – 579 likes and 40 comments*

"Deleted a prior post which I generally oppose doing. But people were being a bit too rude to one another in that stream. Opinions are great but PLEASE voice them appropriately without trying to take other people down. We have ALL ages of fans on here and want this to be a respectful place, regardless of which side of the fence your opinion may rest. Will only mediate when necessary and still holds true—just felt it necessary. Still love you all. Carry on!" *July 30, 2012 – Scene75 – 453 likes and 38 comments*

"Kathleen (our Facebook VIP who always throws in a 'he's cute' comment) stopped in for a drink last night on my bartending shift. How fun!" *August 8, 2012 – Scene75 – 187 likes and 19 comments*

"I was half way out of the parking lot last night when my team informed me that someone wanted to shake my hand to bring in his 30th birthday. Honored to have Dennis WANT to spend #30 with us and to meet me in the process—I'll be following his lead here soon on the birthday business. Thanks Dennis. I was going to guess 6'9" —not too far off! 'Jonah, thanks for taking a moment to meet me last night. Me and my friends had a blast; next time we'll have to get there a little earlier for the bouncy area (yes, my adult friends were upset that they missed it). But the laser tag and go-karts were awesome, even more so because I'm 6'7" and fit in the kart just fine! You did good bringing this place to Dayton, and I hope that it continues to grow. Thanks for helping me bring in the big 3-0!" *August 19, 2012 – Scene75 – 188 likes and 22 comments*

"Thank you so much for putting it all on the line and opening this fantastic family facility. I hope to spend lot$ and lot$ and lot$ of $$$$ there this winter … " *August 22, 2012 – Theresa M.*

"Tonight hubby and I had date night at Scene75. We had dinner … walked around a bit, played a couple of games … til I got hooked on the coin game. Uh-oh … I sent hubby over to reload my card two times … until he said ummmm I don't think so … I am taking your card. Whatttttttt … no fair … but but but … nope he said … so out the door we went … thanks for a great date night, Jonah … " *January 12, 2013 – Tammie W.*

"Big news! Scene75 is going places. Literally! Say hello to our newest family member, the Scene75 Party Bus. Fun graphics to come." *February 6, 2013 – Scene75 – 318 likes and 39 comments*

"And here we GrOw! We are adding another 70 parking spaces, to be ready for the summer … " *February 25, 2013 – Scene75 – 252 likes and 22 comments*

"Scene75 in St. Thomas, USVI. Fan of the year or what?" *March 24, 2013 – Jason A.*

"It's here!!" *April 11, 2013 – Scene75 – 438 likes, 37 comments and 20 shares*

"Nearly one year ago, as we prepared to open Scene75, I called each incoming team member of Scene75 to introduce myself while personally inviting them to join the team. Today I began  the great honor of writing personal thank you notes to each and every teammate who has been with us from the start. Quite a few more letters to go! (Hand starting to get tired. Lol.) Thankful to have such a great team supporting me and the community from day one ... " *May 19, 2013 – Scene75 – 247 likes and 27 comments*

 "The team surprised us at the airport. Picked us up w balloons, a handmade sign, a megaphone and a Scene75 cheer. Winners! IAAPA Brass Ring Awards 2013!"
November 21, 2013 – Scene75 – 102 likes and 5 comments

Appendix: What is Scene75 Entertainment Center?

Located one exit south of the I-70, I-75 highway interchange in Dayton, Ohio, Scene75 Entertainment Center is the largest indoor entertainment center in the United States. Scene75 features a full-service restaurant, two indoor bars, an outdoor patio and bar, the larger of only two indoor electric go-kart tracks in the state of Ohio, the largest multilevel laser tag arena in the tri-state area, the largest indoor bouncing inflatable arena in Ohio, the largest redemption and video arcade in Dayton, twelve first-in-the-country Chaos Room video gaming theater screens, two 4-D theaters with blizzard and wind effects, four mini-bowling lanes, a ten-car bumper car system, 18 holes of black light glow-in-the-dark miniature golf, three outdoor sand volleyball courts, two outdoor bocce courts, a concession stand, and eight private party rooms. In addition to serving daily entertainment, Scene75 hosts more than a thousand birthday parties and corporate events each year.

To learn more about Scene75, please visit or contact us:

Scene75 Entertainment Center

6196 Poe Avenue

Dayton, OH 45414

www.scene75.com

www.facebook.com/scene75

937-619-3200